Dearest F

From one ∧

another.

Love, Robert x

DUMBLEDORE IS SO GAY

A play by Robert Holtom

Published by Playdead Press 2020

© Robert Holtom 2020

Robert Holtom has asserted his rights under the
Copyright, Design and Patents Act, 1988, to be
identified as the author of this work.

A CIP catalogue record for this book is available from
the British Library.

ISBN 978-1-910067-86-4

Playdead Press
www.playdeadpress.com

Dumbledore Is So Gay by Robert Holtom was first performed at the Network Theatre, VAULT Festival, London in February 2020 with the following cast:

CAST

Jack	**Alex Britt**
Gemma | Sally | Madame Dubois Students | STI Guy | Vicar	**Charlotte Dowding**
Ollie | Martin | Guy | Students Banker Guy | Harry Potter Guy	**Max Percy**

CREATIVE TEAM

Writer	**Robert Holtom**
Director	**Tom Wright**
Composer	**Peter Wilson**
Lighting Designer	**Rory Beaton**
Movement Director	**Rachael Nanyonjo**
Producer	**Natalie Chan**

Cover design by James Holtom
Cover image by Gabriel Moake

CAST

ALEX BRITT

Alex is a London-based actor and writer, originally from Gloucestershire. He has trained with The Actor's Class and NYT.

Theatre credits include: *My Dad's Gap Year* (Park Theatre); *Corpus Christi* (Arcola Theatre); *Man-Cub* (Etcetera Theatre, King's Head Theatre); *Fleeced* (The Bread & Roses Theatre, Space Arts Centre); *Our Big Love Story* (The Hope Theatre, Courtyard Theatre); *This Queer House* (Theatre Peckham); *Teeth 'n' Smiles* (LOST Theatre); *Dry Run* (Baron's Court Theatre); *Sleepwalkers* (Edinburgh Fringe Festival); *The Tempest* (The Lion and Unicorn Theatre); *Lysistrata – The Sex Strike* (The Lion and Unicorn Theatre) and *You Can* (National Youth Theatre, Ambassador's Theatre).

Alex also wrote and performed in *Blank Page* for the Actor Awareness LGBTQ+ New Writing Scratch Night.

TV and Film credits include: *EastEnders* (BBC); *Stutter* (Team Angelica); *Nice to Meet You, Florence!* (Counter Film Productions) and *Pendulum* (Trancentry Productions).

CHARLOTTE DOWDING

Charlotte graduated from Mountview in 2017. Other training includes GSA, National Youth Theatre and The BRIT School.

Credits include: *Totally Together* (T.I.E.); *Splintered* (Edinburgh Fringe, VAULT Festival); *Girl Scouts vs. Aliens*

(Edinburgh Fringe); *Eat Your Heart Out* (Edinburgh Fringe, Oxford Fire Station); *Paper. Scissors. Stone.* (VAULT Festival, Elevator Festival); *Common Ground* (Etcetera Theatre); *Commercial Break* (Theatre 503) and *The Taming of the Shrew* (Brockley Jack).

MAX PERCY

Max Percy trained at East15 Acting School, the London School of Russian Classical Ballet and is the Artistic Director of Contingency Theatre.

Acting credits include: *The Disruptors* (Feature Film); *Freedom Hi* (VAULT); *GEORGE* (National Tour); *My Mind is Free* (National Tour); *Tainted* (Short Film); *My Dad's Gap Year* (Park Theatre); *Peter Pan* (Regent's Park Open Air Theatre).

CREATIVE

ROBERT HOLTOM | WRITER

Robert is a playwright, short story writer and narrative coach.

Writing credits include: *The Quest* (Arcola); *The Cluedo Club Killings* (King's Head Theatre, Arcola, Le Funambule Montmartre); *The Wellington Boot Club, The Last Tutorial, Isobel* (Burton Taylor Studio). Short work includes: *Fat* (The Bread & Roses Theatre) and *Having A Ball* (The North Wall).

TOM WRIGHT | DIRECTOR

Tom is a London-based theatre director, playwright and producer, originally from Coventry. He is the New Works Associate at Kiln Theatre having previously been Head of Artist Development at The Old Vic. His two back-to-back debut plays were nominated for seven Off West End Awards including Best New Play and Most Promising Playwright.

Directing credits include: *Blowhole* (Brighton Fringe, Tristan Bates Theatre) and *Tumble Tuck* (King's Head Theatre, Underbelly Edinburgh, Soho Theatre and Old Vic New Voices). Associate credits include: *Legendary Children* (Theatre De Meervaart) and *2.1* (Rich Mix, Camden People's Theatre).

Writing credits include: *Undetectable* (King's Head Theatre); *My Dad's Gap Year* (Park Theatre); *I Ain't Dumb* (Theatre Royal Stratford East) and *Rebel Song* (The Other Palace).

Short work includes: *Broadcast* (Old Vic New Voices); *Three Sunrises* (The Other Palace) and *I, We, Me* (VAULT).

PETER WILSON | COMPOSER

Peter Wilson is a composer for theatre, film, and concert hall.

Theatre as composer includes: productions at the National Theatre, The Old Vic, Donmar, Soho, RADA, The Bunker, and The Vault. In 2017, he was nominated for an Off-West End Award for Best Sound Design. More recently, he won an Olivier Award for Outstanding Achievement in an Affiliate Theatre as one of the creatives on *Flesh and Bone* (Soho).

His other composer credits include: the Royal Northern Sinfonia, Loré Lixenberg, Ligeti Quartet, Norrbotten NEO, Ensemble 360 and Gildas Quartet. He is currently an *'emerging composer'* supported by the Royal Philharmonic Society and, in 2020, will compose a piece for Music in the Round. His compositions have been recorded and released by NMC Recordings. He is an Associate Composer of the University of York Music Press.

Peter has worked professionally as a dancer and choreographer of contemporary ballet. He graduated from The Australian Ballet School in 2010, and subsequently performed in productions across Australia, the USA, Canada, UK and Germany.

RORY BEATON | LIGHTING DESIGNER

Rory was nominated for a 2018 Knight of Illumination Award for his work on *Così fan Tutte* at Opera Holland Park. In 2016 he was awarded the Michael Northen Award by the Association of Lighting Designers.

Credits include: *Kiss Me, Kate* (Watermill); *The Rise and Fall of Little Voice, Summer Holiday* (Octagon); *Così fan Tutte, Rigoletto, L'arlesiana, Manon Lescaut* (Opera Holland Park); *Lovely Ugly City* (Almeida); West End Producer – *Free Willy!* (Cuffe & Taylor); *70 Års Opera* (Danish National Opera); *Edward II* (Arts Theatre, Cambridge); *Dishoom!* (UK Tour); *Dubliners* (OTC Ireland); *Macbeth, Idomeneo, Elizabeth I, The Marriage of Figaro, Gianni Schicchi, Il Tabarro, Radamisto, Dido and Aeneas* (English Touring Opera); *The Blonde Bombshells of 1943, Summer Holiday, A Christmas Carol* (Pitlochry Festival Theatre); *How Love is Spelt* (Southwark); *Skylight* (UK Tour); *Mysterious Bruises* (RADA); *Der Freischütz* (Blackheath Community Opera); *Betty Blue Eyes, L'incoronazione di Poppea* (Trinity Laban); *Maklena* (UK Tour); *Tumble Tuck* (King's Head); *Rigoletto, La Scala di Seta, Riders to the Sea, Il Campanello, The Bear* (Wexford Festival Opera); *Boat, The Best Day Ever* (Company 3); *Fame!, Rent, Legally Blonde, Cats* (Albany, Coventry); *Little Shop of Horrors, Earthquakes in London* (LAMDA); *The Tempest* (Scottish Youth Theatre); *Così fan Tutte* (Guildhall); *Le Nozze di Figaro* (Royal College of Music); *Tell Us Who We Are* (Y-Dance).

RACHAEL NANYONJO | MOVEMENT DIRECTOR

Rachael has a BA Honours in Dance Studies from Roehampton University and an MA in Choreography from Middlesex University.

Choreography & Movement Direction credits include: *The Spine* (20 Stories High – Unity Theatre, Stratford Circus); *In A Word* (Young Vic); *Great Expectations* (National Youth Theatre – Southwark Playhouse); *Either* (Hampstead); *Two Trains Running* (ETT – Royal and Derngate); *American Dream* (Young Vic); *Does My Bomb Look Big In This* (Soho Theatre, Tara Arts); *Babylon Beyond Borders* (The Bush Theatre); *Macbeth* (Orange Tree); *The Jumper Factory* (The Young Vic, Bristol Old Vic); *Misty* (Trafalgar Studios); Olivier Award Nominated, *Sleeping Beauty* (Theatre Royal Stratford East); Black British Theatre Award Best Choreographer Nominated, *After It Rains* (National Youth Theatre); *Shebeen* (Nottingham Playhouse, Theatre Royal Stratford East); *Bernstein's Mass* (Royal Festival Hall, Southbank Centre); *Twilight* (Gate Theatre); *The Divide, Cover My Tracks* (Old Vic).

Directing credits include: *Freedom Project* (Young Vic); *Bobsleigh* (Old Vic Monologues); *Amazina* (Film); *An Alternative Musical* (National Theatre, for NT Learning as co-director); *Assata – She Who Struggles* (Young Vic, for Young Vic fresh direction); *2:1* (Kanzaze Dance Theatre at Rich Mix).

Associate Director credits: *Moonlight/Night School* (Pinter Theatre. Associate to Lyndsey Turner & Ed Stambollouian); *Pericles Public Acts first stage* (National Theatre).

Assistant Director: *The Step Mother* (Chichester Festival Theatre, dir. Richard Eyre); *Caroline Or Change* (Chichester, dir. Michael Longhurst); *Underwater Love* (Arcola, Clapham Omnibus, dir. Caroline Bryant); *Kayla* (Young Vic, dir. Justin Audibert).

NATALIE CHAN | PRODUCER

Natalie is a London based producer, originally from Hong Kong. She trained as Resident Assistant Producer at Theatre503 and worked with The Coronet Theatre, Pleasance Theatre, Invisible Flock, Laughing Horse Comedy and Hong Kong Fringe Club. She is currently a young producer with Battersea Arts Centre. *Dumbledore Is So Gay* is the first theatrical production where Natalie is lead producer.

Assistant credits include: *The Green Fairy* (Union Theatre); Borderline Confrontational's *Godspell* (Edinburgh Fringe Festival); *Bring The Happy* (UK Tour) and *Melbourne International Comedy Festival Roadshow* (Hong Kong part of Asia tour).

WRITER'S NOTE:

It ain't easy being Jack because it isn't always easy being gay. There's sometimes prejudice, indifference and loneliness. But there is also magic, joy and belonging. So I put all these things into a story in the hope that we can have less hate and more love in the years to come.

For Polly Higgins

CHARACTERS:

Jack

Ollie (Jack's best friend)

Gemma (Jack's friend)

Sally (Jack's Mum)

Martin (Jack's Dad)

Madame DuBois (teacher)

Students

Vicar

Men: *Guy, Banker Guy, STI Guy, Harry Potter Guy*

ACT 1

JACK: You know in the Prisoner of Azkaban when Hermione's all super stressed about her homework and Harry and Ron are like *whatevs*, and then Hagrid's favourite hippogriff, Buckbeak, is gonna get the chop? Then Dumbledore says to Hermione "three turns should do it, I think" and, holy hell, she's got a Time Turner! A Time Turner! She's been using it to travel back in time and get to as many lessons as possible because... she's like that. So they go back in time to save Buckbeak and Hagrid is over the moon and it's brilliant.

I'd love a Time Turner. I'd go back and there's so much I'd change. Like. Everything.

I'm Jack by the way and I quite like Harry Potter. Dumbledore's my favourite character because... well, you'll find out. Yeah, I'm Jack and...

School.

...I'm 12 and I hate French. Madame DuBois hasn't arrived yet. The classroom's rammed and the kids are...

STUDENTS: That pencil case is well gay.

Your face is gay.

Your Mum is gay

14

Your Dad's gay, with the milkman.

We don't have a milkman.

Postman?

JACK: And all together now: "Gay!"

MME DUBOIS: Mes enfants, silence s'il vous plait.

OLLIE: (*whispering*) Madame DuBois is gay.

JACK: Well gay.

OLLIE: Gay with the head cook.

JACK: They eat lasagne off each other's tits.

OLLIE: Gross.

JACK: And lick each other's...

MME DUBOIS: Children, silence!

JACK: Ollie's sitting in front of me, he's my best mate, we've known each other forever. He's as bored as I am and starts staring out the window. He's got nice cheeks and his nose...it's like a ski jump, a very tiny ski jump. It's the best nose ever.

MME DUBOIS: Oliver! Eyes to ze front!

JACK: And I've got a boner. Full hard on in my pants. I'm getting a lot more boners these days, it's well awkward.

Home. The TV is on.

15

JACK: This is my Mum, Sally.

SALLY: Oo, I do like her jumper, I wonder where she got it from.

JACK: And this is my Dad, Martin.

MARTIN: Mmm.

JACK: And we're watching telly. Simple right?

SALLY: I just don't get it, why did she try to burn down the pub?

MARTIN: Mmm.

SALLY: It was a question Martin.

MARTIN: The insurance money.

SALLY: But her name's not on the deed.

MARTIN: Her husband will get the money.

SALLY: But they hate each other.

MARTIN: I dunno, stop blethering.

SALLY: Maybe she's going to kill her husband.

The next show begins.

MARTIN: Change over.

SALLY: Why?

MARTIN: I don't want to watch this.

16

SALLY: It's just Graham Norton, what's wrong with him?

MARTIN: Well, he's…

SALLY: What?

MARTIN: He's a poof.

SALLY: Martin, he's just Irish.

MARTIN: Sally, he's… he's a gay.

SALLY: I think he's just one of those overly friendly, well-groomed men.

MARTIN: Just change over.

JACK: (*to audience*) A few nights later and I have Ollie and Gemma over. She's my other best mate. We've got popcorn and *The Prisoner of Azkaban*, it's one of the…

GEMMA: …worst!

OLLIE: No, that's *The Chamber of Secrets*, with the dumbass snake.

JACK: It's a Basilisk actually and this one's a classic.

GEMMA: I think classic and Harry Potter in the same sentence…

JACK: Are like salt and vinegar crisps with Diet Coke.

OLLIE: Mmm, tasty.

17

JACK:	(*to audience*) Look, there's something I need to tell you before we go on, it's kinda like a confession. I... I am... a Hufflepuff. I know, I know, totally lame, if you didn't like me at the start you're not gonna like me now. I really wanted to be in Gryffindor with Harry, Ron and Hermione but I got sorted into Huffletwat and there's nothing I could do about it. Oh, and my Patronus is a hedgehog. An actual hedgehog.
GEMMA:	Can't we watch something else? I'd settle for *Die Hard*.
OLLIE:	That's a Christmas movie.
GEMMA:	From the guy who watches *Love Actually* all year round.
OLLIE:	That's supposed to be a secret.
JACK:	Shh, it's about to start.
OLLIE:	Where's the popcorn?
GEMMA:	I've got it!

Ollie reaches over Jack to get the popcorn. Jack inhales.

JACK:	Lynx Apollo, my favourite. (*he looks down at his crotch in shock*) It's happening again! (*he jumps up*).
OLLIE:	Jesus!
GEMMA:	Jack!

18

JACK:	Sorry, more volume.
GEMMA:	Use the remote.
JACK:	Where is it?
OLLIE:	In your hand.

Bedroom.

JACK: Once Ollie and Gemma have gone I creep into the kitchen and take a copy of Mum's Cosmo and one of Dad's Men's Health. I sneak back to my room. (*He puts the magazines on the floor in front of him*). This is it.

He opens Cosmopolitan and looks at some of the pictures of the women. Then he does the same for Men's Health. His eyes linger. He holds it up to get a better look and then drops it. He starts to cry.

School.

OLLIE: Haven't you heard?

JACK: What?

OLLIE: About Dumbledore?

JACK: No.

OLLIE: He's gay.

JACK: (*to audience*) Of course I know, that was revealed on Friday 19th October, 2007. Three years ago!

(*to Ollie*) You're joking?

OLLIE: No, he's totally gay. He doesn't look gay though, does he?

JACK: What?

OLLIE: Well, gays look like fairies, like that old Norman who lives down Bridge Road.

JACK: Not old Norman?

OLLIE: My brother calls him a bender. Says he takes it up the poohole.

JACK: Gross!

OLLIE: He's an old creep.

JACK: Yeah.

(*to audience*) I quite like old Norman actually, he always says hello.

(*to Ollie*) He's a total weirdo.

OLLIE: Poof.

JACK: Fag.

OLLIE: Oi! Who you calling a fag!

JACK: Nah, I mean old Norman...

Ollie puts Jack in a headlock.

OLLIE: You're the fag!

JACK: No I'm not!

OLLIE: Bender.

The sound of a school corridor.

JACK: When you pour hydro-sulphuric acid onto a wet sponge it melts into this fizzing, bubbling, black mess.

STUDENTS: That's well gay.

You're gay!

Poof.

JACK: And that's what it's like, like someone pouring hydro-sulphuric acid onto me.

STUDENTS: Butt muncher.

Fudge packer.

Chocolate chomper.

Liquorice licker.

JACK: But I can't scream because then they'd pour it down my throat. So I keep my mouth shut for years and let them bully Jizzy Joe instead.

At the swimming pool, four years later.

JACK: Four years later, I'm sixteen now.

OLLIE: Mate, there's no dispute, your front crawl is awful.

JACK: Cheers.

OLLIE: What's your top score?

JACK:	What?
OLLIE:	On Coin Crunchers.
JACK:	16,000.
OLLIE:	Mate, you've not got 16,000, there aren't even that many coins.
JACK:	Yeah there are, you've got to get to the secret waterfall level.
OLLIE:	Fuck the secret waterfall level. Did you hear about old Norman? One of his windows got smashed.
JACK:	How did that happen?
OLLIE:	Can you keep a secret?
JACK:	Yeah.
OLLIE:	Mikey…
JACK:	(*to audience*) That's Ollie's older brother
OLLIE:	…and one of his mates threw a brick at it.
JACK:	Why?
OLLIE:	Coz he's a fag, isn't he.
JACK:	Your brother could get arrested.
OLLIE:	No he won't, he's done the world a favour.

Pause.

OLLIE:	I wonder what it's like though.

22

JACK:	What?
OLLIE:	Taking it up the bum.
JACK:	(*to audience*) For AS levels I do Geography, Maths and English.
GEMMA:	Jack, it's not that hard, you just have to see it a bit like a poem.
JACK:	I don't like poems.
GEMMA:	Then why did you choose English?
JACK:	Ollie said it's a doss.
GEMMA:	Ollie's an idiot.
JACK:	True. But why can't this be in proper English?
GEMMA:	It's Shakespeare! He pretty much invented the language. Have you at least read the Spark Notes?
JACK:	Yeah.
GEMMA:	So you know Romeo and Juliet get together.
JACK:	Yeah.
GEMMA:	Yeah.

Gemma leans across the table and kisses Jack. She quickly leans back. Jack is stunned.

GEMMA:	Are you alright?
JACK:	Yeah.

GEMMA:	Can we do that again?
JACK:	Yeah.
	(*to audience*) And about a week later it's official.
OLLIE:	You and Gemma!?
JACK:	Yeah.
OLLIE:	You *and* Gemma?
JACK:	Yes.
OLLIE:	You and... Hermione!?

Pause.

	What's it like?
JACK:	What?
OLLIE:	Magaluf.
JACK:	What?
OLLIE:	Her pussy, what's her pussy like?
JACK:	Oh. Er, we haven't done it...
OLLIE:	Mate, what are you waiting for? Has she at least tossed you off?
JACK:	Er...
OLLIE:	She's made you cum?
JACK:	Yeah.

OLLIE: Was it good?

JACK: Great.

OLLIE: Did you cum a lot or a little? Like a fountain or a puddle?

JACK: Mate!

OLLIE: I still can't believe you haven't banged her, get in there!

GEMMA: (*on phone to a friend*) The turquoise one, are you sure? It's not too... well, y'know... desperate? ...I know, I know, I'm a powerful, beautiful woman. I'm a powerful, beautiful woman. Right? ...Yup, you're right, deep breath. I just, I... I'm dead nervous. I really don't want it to hurt too much. I hope I'm good, I don't want him to get bored... I know, powerful, beautiful, powerful, beautiful...

Gemma and Jack sit next to one another awkwardly.

JACK: Are you sure?

GEMMA: I'm sure.

JACK: Or some orange juice?

GEMMA: I'm fine, Jack.

JACK: Ribena?

GEMMA: No.

JACK: Just tap water then?

GEMMA: Jack!

They sit awkwardly for longer until Jack puts his hand on Gemma's thigh, they lean in to kiss again.

GEMMA: (*on phone to a friend, she's crying*) I... I... I don't want to talk about it. I... I...

Jack is sitting with Sally.

SALLY: These things don't always work out, love, especially not when you're young. Your Dad and I had to learn a lot of things the hard way, it wasn't always easy, but now look at us, a lovely house and a special boy. You'll have this too one day, a home, a family. Just you wait.

JACK: Can I tell you something?

SALLY: Course love, what is it?

JACK: It's... I'm...

SALLY: Yeah?

JACK: Going to bed.

SALLY: It's only 7, love, *Eastenders* will be on soon.

JACK: (*to audience*) You know Dumbledore dies, right? Spoilers. Snape zaps him off the Astronomy Tower and when he hits the ground he breaks every bone in his body. So the only gay character in the Harry Potter series dies. It's shit isn't it.

Behind the swimming pool.

OLLIE: (*choking*) I fucking hate fags. But Mikey says I've got to get good at smoking, all the lads do it.

JACK: (*to audience*) We're in the middle of A2s. Even worse than AS.

(*to Ollie*) Let me try.

OLLIE: Nah, you can't handle it.

JACK: Don't be a dick.

Ollie holds the cigarette up for Jack and moves it towards his mouth. His fingers brush his lips and they stare at each other. Ollie leans in and they kiss. It lasts for a few seconds before Ollie backs off.

JACK: (*to audience*) I feel his lips on mine for days, that kiss is everything. I even buy a can of Lynx Apollo, the smell makes me dizzy. He avoids me for two weeks but then the footy's on at The Old Rose and...

Pub.

JACK: Goal!!!

OLLIE: Epic!

JACK: Did you see that?

OLLIE: No mate, I was knitting.

JACK: Headed it like a boss.

OLLIE: Like a boss.

JACK: (*to audience*) We leave the pub together and stagger home. It's not suspicious because everyone knows we're best mates. But halfway through the park he grabs me and says...

OLLIE: Kiss me.

JACK: What?

OLLIE: Kiss me again...

They kiss. They start feeling one another's bodies. Jack moves his hand down towards Ollie's crotch and Ollie shoves him back.

OLLIE: Fuck off, don't touch my dick.

JACK: Mate, sorry...

OLLIE: It's gay.

JACK: All of this gay.

OLLIE: I'm not gay. You're the fag.

JACK: (*to audience*) We do this on and off for a while, drunk kissing. It's not exactly how I imagined but I love it. And I start to love him. I see it all: our first Katie Perry concert, holiday in Mykonos and one day I'll propose. He's the one. He's the one I've been waiting for.

The sound of zombies.

We're at his one night after exams. I got two Ds and a C, by the way. He's nabbed a bottle of his Mum's vodka and we shot every time a zombie bites someone.

The sound of someone screaming, they shot.

We're wasted!

Another scream, another shot.

And then...

They start to kiss, the kiss intensifies, but then the sound of a door opening, they scramble away from each other, they're caught.

SALLY: Calm down Martin!

MARTIN: I will not fu...effing calm down. A...a...poof, in my own house!

SALLY: Don't call him that.

MARTIN: How long have you known?

SALLY: Of course I didn't know, he was with Gemma before.

MARTIN: Yeah, and what happened to her?

SALLY: She's long gone.

MARTIN: You should have been stricter with him. You were always letting him and that Ollie play together.

SALLY: Don't blame this on me. Maybe if you did more than sit around watching telly...

JACK: *(to audience)* It was Mikey who caught us. He punched Ollie in the face and threw me out the house.

(on phone) Ollie, please call me back, just let me know you're OK. I miss you.

Ollie, hello. Come on, mate, I'm really worried.

Mate, send me a snapchat or something, anything.

(to audience) He ends up blocking me on all social media and I get a job at the local Tesco's.

The sound of shopping items being beeped at a checkout.

ANNOUNCER: Clean-up on Aisle 3 please, clean-up on Aisle 3.

Gemma approaches the checkout with her shopping.

JACK: Hi.

GEMMA: Hi.

Pause.

JACK: How are you?

GEMMA: How do you think I am, Jack?

JACK: I dunno.

GEMMA: You should have told me.

JACK: What?

GEMMA: That you're gay.

Pause.

What you did to me... it was sick.

JACK: Gemma, I'm sorry.

GEMMA: It's too late for that.

JACK: I'm sorry.

GEMMA: I hate you.

JACK: (*to audience*) He comes in one day. There's a giant shiner on his left cheek, he's still beautiful though. But when he sees me he turns and leaves, I think he shops at LIDL after that. Sometimes when I'm in my room at night and I can't sleep I imagine climbing to the top of the Astronomy Tower, wind rushing through my hair, some hippogriff flying in the distance above the Black Lake and...

Sally and Martin are mid-argument.

MARTIN: We went for a day's hiking in the Brecon Beacons, Sally. He got blisters and I fell in a ditch. There was no time for the birds and the bees. What about your trip to Chessington?

SALLY: Chessington!? Chessington! World of flipping adventures. I was too busy trying not to be sick on that stupid swinging ship thing. The Talk is your job.

MARTIN: My job!? You're his mother.

SALLY: And you're the one with a... with a... penis. You're the one that has to show him how to be a man.

MARTIN: What's that supposed to mean?

SALLY: It means neither of us ever spoke to him. So he probably just got it all from google.

MARTIN: There's all sorts on the internet!

SALLY: Exactly.

MARTIN: My Dad never gave me the talk.

SALLY: Your Dad barely talked at all he drank so much.

MARTIN: Don't start on that.

SALLY: I just don't get it, Jack's a good lad, why does he want to make his life harder for himself? (*she breaks*).

MARTIN: Sally... come on... how about I make us a cup of tea?

JACK: (*to audience*) Then one day, I'm just like, fuck it. I nick £50 out my Dad's wallet, get on the Megabus to London and that night I find...

32

The sound of cheesy pop music, a pumping bass, flashing lights, Jack is in G-A-Y Heaven.

JACK: Heaven, actual heaven! It's a haze of smoke machines, sweat, Gogo boys, dripping walls and a million shards of disco ball. There are guys everywhere. Tall guys, short guys, muscular, hairy, bald, and they're all gay!

GUY: Hi handsome.

JACK: (*to audience*) Hot! Pecs you could impale yourself on.

GUY: I'm Guy, you having fun?

JACK: Yeah. I... I'm Jack.

GUY: You're cute.

JACK: Thanks. Er, what do you do?

GUY: I'm a vlogger. Have we spoken on Grindr?

JACK: No.

GUY: What are you into?

JACK: JD and Coke?

(*to audience*). He pulls me to the dance floor and presses his body against mine. He leans in and kisses me. He uses a lot of tongue, like, a lot, he even puts it in my ear. Then he licks his finger, slips it under my pants and puts it in my bum. He didn't ask if he could do that and I didn't ask him to. I don't know if I like it. I mean, I didn't want a finger in my bum. I just freeze.

So I work during the week and avoid my parents, then come Saturday, Heaven. Sometimes I go back to guys' places, it's fun. I get with a banker...

BANKER GUY: Give it to me, ugh, give it to me like a sub-prime mortgage.

JACK: (*to audience*) ...and a guy with...

STI GUY: Syphilis.

JACK: What?

STI GUY: Yeah, I've got syphilis.

JACK: Could you maybe have told me that before we... y'know.

(*to audience*) ...and one guy's really into Harry Potter, like *really* into Harry Potter...

POTTER GUY: You must be Hufflepuff!

JACK: No way, I'm Gryffindor.

POTTER GUY: I got Slytherin, can't argue with the Sorting Hat. What's your Patronus?

JACK: A wolf.

POTTER GUY: Nice! Mines an otter, cute right. Can I wear a gown?

JACK: What?

POTTER GUY: When we do it, can I wear a gown? Harry Potter's my kink.

JACK: (*to audience*) Jack pot!

Then one night, when I'm staggering out of Heaven I get a call from an unsaved number...

Hello?

Silence.

Hello, is anyone there?

OLLIE: Jack.

JACK: Ollie, is that you?

Silence.

JACK: Are you OK?

OLLIE: Jack, I...

JACK: What? Where are you?

OLLIE: I miss you.

The line goes dead.

(*to audience*) I ring back but he never picks up. I hear some guy gets acid chucked in his face outside a gay club in Vauxhall. London is fucking bonkers. Then one Sunday afternoon when I get home, hanging like a dog, Mum's waiting for me at the kitchen table. I try to avoid her but...

35

SALLY:	Jack, we need to talk.
JACK:	No we don't.
SALLY:	It's serious.
JACK:	Mum, I'm eighteen, I can do what I want. I know you and Dad hate it
SALLY:	Jack...
JACK:	But when I've got the cash I'm out of here.
SALLY:	Jack, just sit down. Please.

Jack sits.

SALLY:	There's something I need to tell you.
JACK:	What?
SALLY:	It's... it's Ollie.
JACK:	What about him?
SALLY:	I don't know how to... he... he's died.

Pause.

SALLY:	He... he killed himself.
JACK:	No. You're lying.
SALLY:	I wish...
JACK:	Stop being a bitch.
SALLY:	Jack, he's gone. Barbara's distraught.
JACK:	How?

SALLY: I don't know, I didn't want to ask.

JACK: You're lying.

Early morning Trafalgar Square traffic.

JACK: One Sunday morning and I'm sat on a bench in Trafalgar Square, my head spinning from poppers. The traffic lights are all green and the night buses are speeding past.

I can't believe he did it. He's dead. He must have been terrified, and so sad. No, not sad, desolate. He was meant to be the one. The love of my life.

And he will be. I'm going to go back and I'm going to save him because we're meant to be together.

Silence. He takes out his Time Turner.

JACK: Three turns should do it, I think.

ACT 2

School.

JACK: I hate French.

STUDENTS: Gay, gay, gay, gay, gay.

JACK: Gay.

MME DUBOIS: Silence, mes enfants!

STUDENTS: (*whispering*) Madame DuBois is well ugly.

Like the head cook.

They're shagging.

Gross!

MME DUBOIS: Children, silence!

JACK: It's perfect, like a ski jump for ants.

MME DUBOIS: Eyes front, Oliver!

JACK: Oh shit... boner!

Home, TV.

SALLY: Wait a sec, if Stella robbed the deli why did the money end up in Madge's chest of drawers.

MARTIN: I haven't a clue.

The next show starts.

MARTIN: Why does he always have to rub it in our faces? I pay taxes for this.

| SALLY: | He could tone it down a bit. |

Harry Potter with Gemma and Ollie.

JACK:	(*to audience*) *The Goblet of Fire!* I'm Gryffindor by the way, got sorted there my first time. What? I did.
OLLIE:	She's well hot in this one.
GEMMA:	Please, she's so obnoxious with all her books and top marks.
OLLIE:	Oh obnoxious is she! Pot...
JACK:	Kettle...
GEMMA:	Twats. Can't we watch something else? Even *The Lord of the Rings*.
OLLIE:	At least this one doesn't have that stupid snake in it.
JACK:	I think you'll find it's a Basilisk.
OLLIE:	Well look at you Mister...
JACK:	Shh, it's...
OLLIE:	Popcorn please!

Ollie reaches over, Jack inhales then lurches forward.

| JACK: | Volume! |

Bedroom, Jack is reading Men's Health

JACK:	Orlando Bloom's in this one, with his top off. He's got a six-pack to grate cheese on. Shit. I am so...

School.

OLLIE:	...gay, Dumbledore is *so* gay.
JACK:	No way!?
OLLIE:	He's like that old Norman, Mum says she saw him holding hands with a man once.
JACK:	Really?
OLLIE:	Yeah, Mikey shouted bender at him the other day.
JACK:	Why?
OLLIE:	I dunno, he just did.
JACK:	That's not very nice.
OLLIE:	It was just a joke.
JACK:	Your brother's a twat.
OLLIE:	Piss off!

Pause.

JACK:	What would you do though, if you found out someone you knew was gay?
OLLIE:	What, like my brother?
JACK:	Lol.

OLLIE: Or my friend?

Pause.

JACK: I'm not gay.

OLLIE: I didn't say you are.

JACK: You're gay.

OLLIE: No I'm not.

Awkward silence as they stare at each other.

The sound of a school corridor.

JACK: Silkworms eat mulberry leaves, loads and loads of mulberry leaves, then they spit them back out all over themselves. A cocoon of spit, gross right.

STUDENTS: Rear Admiral.

Bum Bandit.

JACK: But that's what I've got to do, I build an invisible cocoon around myself and hide.

STUDENTS: Butt Gangster.

Willy Warrior.

Dick Diver.

What?

JACK: For years the cocoon grows until…

At the swimming pool.

JACK:	I'm sixteen...
OLLIE:	...20,000 is literally impossible, even with the secret waterfall level.
JACK:	What about the cherry blossom level, full of coins.
OLLIE:	There isn't a cherry blossom level.
JACK:	Wanna bet?
OLLIE:	Give that here...
JACK:	No.
OLLIE:	Give it!
JACK:	Oi!

Ollie snatches the phone out of Jack's hand, as he does the game minimises and the photos come up instead.

OLLIE:	Is that Orlando Bloom?
JACK:	Shit.
OLLIE:	Paddle boarding naked!
JACK:	I'm learning to paddleboard.
OLLIE:	Fuck off. Mate, you *are* gay.
JACK:	No. Yes.
OLLIE:	Mate, you should have told me. Does anyone else know?
JACK:	No.

OLLIE: They'll tear you a new one. Shit, they'll tear *me* a new one.

JACK: What are you talking about?

OLLIE: You know what they're like, the footy guys.

JACK: They're douchebags.

OLLIE: If they know I'm hanging out with a bender.

JACK: Oi, don't call me that.

OLLIE: It'll be the end of me.

JACK: There's nothing wrong with it.

Pause.

Is there?

OLLIE: No, er...

JACK: It's normal, there's nothing wrong with it.

OLLIE: Just keep your mouth shut.

JACK: Most guys fancy other guys.

OLLIE: No they don't.

JACK: They just don't do anything about it.

OLLIE: I don't fancy other guys.

JACK: I've seen the way you look at your teammates.

OLLIE: Fuck off, I am not gay.

JACK:	I didn't say you were gay I just said…
OLLIE:	Fuck off, if you say anything, I'll…
JACK:	What?
OLLIE:	I'll…
JACK:	(*to audience*) …tell the footy team. That's what he does, for lad points.
STUDENTS:	Bum basher!
	Butt bonker.
	Bottom bumper.
JACK:	He might as well have just pushed me off the Astronomy Tower.
STUDENTS:	Cheek chaser.
	Crack climber.
MME DUBOIS:	Children, stop saying such 'orrible things!
STUDENTS:	Hole hunter.
JACK:	So what if I am?

The students start laughing.

Home.

JACK:	I fucking hate the iambic pentameter.
GEMMA:	Jack!

JACK:	I don't care if this line has only nine beats in it.
GEMMA:	Have you at least read the Spark Notes?
JACK:	I can't be bothered.
GEMMA:	Come on, Jack, I thought you used to like English.
JACK:	Used to.
GEMMA:	I know it's hard but you've got to work.
JACK:	You don't have a clue. It's been nearly two years and they still haven't stopped. It's like acid rain.
GEMMA:	I do have a clue actually. Guys are always making jokes about my breasts.
JACK:	That's shit.
GEMMA:	Yeah.
JACK:	Why can't they just bully Jizzy Joe instead?
GEMMA:	No. That's horrible. You can't push someone else under the bus just because you're suffering.
JACK:	Fine. I'm sorry. I just want them to stop.
GEMMA:	I know. Have you talked with your Mum?
JACK:	No.
GEMMA:	She'll understand.

JACK: No she won't, she hates Graham Norton.

GEMMA: Because he's Irish!? Oh...

JACK: He was supposed to be my friend. I hate him.

Pause.

GEMMA: Yeah.

JACK: What?

GEMMA: What?

JACK: What aren't you telling me?

GEMMA: Nothing.

JACK: Bullshit.

Pause.

GEMMA: It's Ollie, he and I are...

JACK: No fucking way.

GEMMA: It's only been a few dates but I think it could be serious.

JACK: You know he's gay.

GEMMA: I don't think so, Jack.

Gemma leaves, Sally arrives.

SALLY: I'm your mother, of course I know when something's up.

JACK: I'm fine.

46

SALLY: No you're not.

JACK: Yes I am.

SALLY: Jack, please, you know you can talk to me
            about anything.

JACK: What if... what if I told you that I don't
            really like girls.

SALLY: What do you mean?

JACK: What if I prefer guys?

Pause

SALLY: Oh Jack, you're too young to know these
            things.

JACK: No I'm not.

SALLY: Are you sure?

JACK: Yes.

SALLY: Do you think maybe it's just a phase?

JACK: No, Mum, I'm... I'm gay.

            (*to audience*) Then the next day at breakfast...

SALLY: Your Dad and I had a chat last night and...
            Martin.

MARIN: Yes?

SALLY: Well, come on, say something.

MARTIN: Yeah, um, well...

SALLY:	Exactly, you're still our son, Jack, whatever you... whoever you are.
JACK:	Thank you.
SALLY:	But we think you should talk to someone.
JACK:	Like who?
SALLY:	Like a doctor.
JACK:	A doctor? I'm not ill.
SALLY:	We just think you should get some help.
MARTIN:	And for God's sake don't tell anyone else, especially not Aunt Brenda.
JACK:	(*to audience*) At school I'm still number one target for bullying but over the years I've mastered the art of self-defence sassery...
STUDENT:	Fag.
JACK:	Needle dick.
STUDENT:	Poof.
JACK:	Look who's talking.
STUDENT:	Ponce.
JACK:	And ten times the man you'll ever be.

(*to audience*) And the cocoon gets thicker until it calcifies, until I can't even find my skin. I get two Cs and a D and a job as pot wash at The Old Rose. People don't speak to me |

48

much, which is better than getting called poof every five minutes. One day Gemma's waiting for me outside the pub.

GEMMA: Hello you.

JACK: Hi.

Pause.

GEMMA: It's been ages, Jack.

JACK: Has it?

GEMMA: We need to do a Harry Potter marathon.

JACK: You always said you hated those.

GEMMA: What about that new *Fantastic Beasts* film, it's coming out soon?

JACK: No comment.

GEMMA: I... er... I miss you. We miss you.

JACK: I miss me too.

     (*to audience*) At home I spend most of my time in my room.

SALLY: I'm worried about him, Martin.

MARTIN: Worried about who?

SALLY: Father Christmas. Jack! Who do you think?

MARTIN: He's a teenager.

SALLY:	He was always so lively when he was little. Remember all those kids' parties, the other children were so dull but Jack just shone.
MARTIN:	He can't be a kid forever.
SALLY:	But the shine's gone out of him. I know it's because he's... well, different. I guess he always was.
MARTIN:	Things might change.
SALLY:	What do you mean?
MARTIN:	Well, when he's a bit older, he might make different choices.
SALLY:	You really think so? Why can't you have a chat with him?
MARTIN:	I don't think so.
SALLY:	Why not? You can't leave me to do it all the time.
MARTIN:	It's... well... it's not my job.
SALLY:	Job! It's not as if I'm getting paid for this.
MARTIN:	I dunno... I... um, my father was never a very chatty man, my mother was the one that did the talking.
JACK:	(*to audience*) Life's about as boring as the first half of *The Order of The Phoenix*, sorry JK, so I save up my pot wash money and one day I get on the Megabus to...

50

The sound of cheesy pop music.

JACK: Heaven! It's amazing. There are Go-go dancers and the toilets stink of cum! There are so many guys here and they're all hanging out together. I'd love that. A group of gay friends, like Harry, Ron and Hermione, but Hermione's an epic lesbian. This guy checks me out and I check him out, it's tense, it's sexy, like this (*he does an impression*). No smiling though, I think this is where smiles go to die. And that night I discover rimming. It's when you lick someone's arsehole or someone licks yours. I love it! Suffice it to say, that's not the only time I go to Heaven...

BANKER GUY: Give it to me, ugh, give it to me like a toxic asset.

STI GUY: Yeah, so syphilis is actually on the rise amongst guys who sleep with guys, we've got to be careful.

POTTER GUY: Could you maybe yell Expecto Patronum when you cum?

JACK: (*to audience*) Then one Sunday afternoon, Mum's waiting for me at the kitchen table.

SALLY: What did you get up to last night?

JACK: Just seeing some friends.

SALLY: Who?

JACK: It doesn't matter.

51

SALLY: You've got to be careful.

Pause

SALLY: There's something I need to tell you. It's very
              sad, Jack.

JACK: What happened to him?

SALLY: Well, I think it was a heart attack or
              something.

JACK: What, Ollie?

SALLY: No, old Norman.

JACK: Oh, shit.

SALLY: Poor man. It's so sad, dying alone. I don't
              want you to end up like him, it's such a lonely
              life. It's just, you've chosen such a difficult
              path.

JACK: I didn't choose anything.

SALLY: What about a girl, Jack, a nice girl to look
              after you. Like Ollie and Gemma, they've
              been going steady for years now. You could
              even have kids one day. You'd make such a
              good father. I just don't want you missing out
              on a happy life.

JACK: (*to audience*) Then a few months later guess
              who I bump into at Heaven? (*to Ollie*) Ollie!

OLLIE: Jack!

JACK: What are you doing here?

Silence. Ollie is about to turn away but Jack takes his arm, gently, and makes him look him in the eye. Ollie leans forward.

OLLIE: I'm so sorry.

JACK: (*to* audience) We go for coffee in this dingy little café that stinks of bacon and he tells me everything...

OLLIE: I left my phone lying around...

GEMMA: When were you going to tell me this, Ollie? Or were you just going to keep sending dick pics to random guys on Grindr behind my back?

OLLIE: She dumped me. I begged her not to tell her mates and in the end she said she wouldn't say anything but she never wants to see me again.

Pause.

               It made me think of what I did to you back at school.

Pause.

               I... I ruined your life.

JACK: Yeah, you did. School was awful because of you.

OLLIE: You didn't deserve any of that.

JACK: (*to audience*) Despite everything, I can't hate him. And I'm doing it...

53

He leans across the table, takes Ollie's chin in his hands and they kiss.

| | And so it begins. We start getting the Megabus together and dance our pants off at Heaven. We hold each other really tight. I feel his chest, his tummy, his back, his neck, his hair, all his body, and it's like home. And one night, when his Mum and brother are away, we sneak back to his and… |

OLLIE: Did you like that? Was I alright? Do you regret it?

JACK: Ollie, are you joking, I've wanted that for years.

OLLIE: I know. Back at school the footy lads had this chant about bashing batty boys, we'd sing it in the changing room before matches, and I had to keep my eyes off their bodies, just concentrate on my locker and sing that stupid fucking song. I was terrified.

JACK: I'm here now.

OLLIE: And did you like my dick? It's kind of a bit curvy. Shit, what was that?

They listen.

JACK: Just the house creaking.

OLLIE: If they find us, we're dead.

JACK: I told my parents eventually, they didn't like it but they've accepted it.

OLLIE: Mikey would flip and Mum would cry, she's always wanted me to be a manly man. Instead she got a fag.

JACK: Don't say that.

OLLIE: Come on, you've seen them at Heaven. Guys are always grabbing my butt, and I swear someone tried to spike my drink last week. Gays are either fucking each other or fucking each other over, any which way a lot of fucking's involved. What sort of Mum wants that for a son? There's something wrong with us, like it's in our DNA.

JACK: Ollie, your DNA is beautiful, it's got nothing to do with genes and everything to do with how they treat us. Years and years of oppression, all that internalised shame, yet somehow they expect us to fit in and "be normal".

OLLIE: I don't deserve you.

JACK: We're together now, that's what counts. That's what all this has been for (*he leans in to kiss Ollie*).

(*to audience*) And one day I invite him over for Sunday lunch.

Home.

SALLY: I hear you're working on reception at the Travel Lodge. How's that?

OLLIE: Y'know, pretty boring, but I'm learning to code.

SALLY: That's good, would you like more roast potatoes?

OLLIE: No thank you, I'm so full...

SALLY: Just a few more.

OLLIE: OK, thanks.

SALLY: I'm sorry things between you and Gemma didn't work out.

OLLIE: Yeah, so am I.

SALLY: Is there anyone new on the horizon.

Pause.

OLLIE: Um, not yet.

SALLY: Bit more gravy?

OLLIE: No, I'm fine... OK, thanks.

JACK: Mum, Dad, there's something I want to tell you (*he looks at Ollie, Ollie shakes his head, he looks terrified*). I... I want more potatoes.

(*to audience*) Heaven keeps calling and we dance till we get blisters. We live for it, it's bliss. Until... What the fuck! What the fuck are you doing?

OLLIE: Nothing, leave off.

JACK: You were kissing him.

OLLIE: It was nothing.

JACK: You had your hands down his pants, that's not nothing.

OLLIE: Stop making a big deal of it.

JACK: But I thought we were boyfriends.

OLLIE: I never said that.

JACK: But all those nights...

OLLIE: I said you deserved better, you should have listened.

JACK: (*to audience*) And that's that, straight off the ski jump and into a tree. He rings me a week later.

OLLIE: I'm so sorry. I shouldn't have kissed that guy, I was wasted.

JACK: That's not an excuse.

OLLIE: I really want to see you again.

JACK: (*to audience*) And I want him, I want him so much, so we try again. And a few weeks later...

(*to Ollie*) You said you'd stopped using Grindr.

OLLIE: I have stopped.

JACK: You were messaging that guy who lives near the pub, weren't you? He sent you dick pics. See!

OLLIE: You're a stalker.

JACK: And you're a fucking liar. You were right, us gays, we're fucked.

(*to audience*) And one night, just before day breaks, I'm sat on a bench in Trafalgar Square and...

He breaks down and starts to cry.

...the tears don't stop. What's the point of this fucking cocoon if on the inside I'm broken?

I've been falling for so long, just like Dumbledore, but now it's time I hit the ground. I'll walk into the middle of the road when the lights are green.

I thought saving Ollie, I thought being with Ollie would make everything better but it didn't because *everything* needs to be better.

I have to change everything and everyone.

The sound of traffic, then silence.

JACK: Three turns should do it, I think.

ACT 3

School.

JACK: French is alright.

STUDENTS: That pencil case is gay.

Glitter is for gays

You're gay.

No I'm not, you're gay.

JACK: And all together now...

MME DUBOIS: Children, shut up! I will not tolerate this awful behaviour anymore. If I 'ear one more slur there will be 'ell to pay. Do you understand me, 'ell!

STUDENTS: Wow.

Wow.

Madame DuBois is...

Fierce.

JACK: His nose. It's everything.

MME DUBOIS: Oliver, a little more attention pleaze.

Home, TV.

SALLY: I'm just saying, if Pam murdered Bob and was back at the pub in time for the party then she ran a mile in under four minutes.

The next show starts.

MARTIN: Oh, change over.

SALLY: Why?

MARTIN: It's that bloody Graham Norton.

SALLY: What's wrong with him?

JACK: Jesus Dad, get a grip.

MARTIN: What!?

JACK: He's gay. Get over it.

SALLY: He's just Irish.

JACK: Mum, he's Irish *and* he's gay.

SALLY: Oh.

JACK: We are not changing over.

They watch.

Harry Potter with Gemma and Ollie.

JACK: *The Order of The Phoenix!*

GEMMA: Boring!

JACK: *(to audience)* I'm Hufflepuff, by the way, a
            proud Puff!

OLLIE: I mean, it is a bit slow.

JACK: *(to audience)* And my Patronus is an ocicat!

OLLIE: Popcorn!

Jack gets awkward and lurches forward.

JACK: Volume!

Bedroom.

JACK: Dad gets me this great book right, it's a bit immature with loads of cartoons but they're funny and a bit adult. There's this one of two boys in the shower and they're both looking at each others' willies. One's circumcised and the other is starting to get pubes. The looks on their faces, priceless! The book doesn't tell me everything I want to know, but it's a start.

School.

JACK: It's tragic.

OLLIE: I couldn't believe it.

JACK: At least he died saving Harry. It pisses me off though, that the only gay character in the entire series dies.

OLLIE: Dumbledore is gay?

JACK: Dumbledore is so gay. JK. outed him yonks ago.

OLLIE: Oh.

JACK: I wish there were more gay characters. Imagine if Harry were gay.

OLLIE: Haha, no way.

JACK: Yeah, and Ron, and they become epic boyfriends.

OLLIE: Mate, keep your voice down, someone will hear you.

JACK: I don't care.

The sounds of a school corridor.

STUDENTS: Ball bouncer.

Dong dinger.

Sack sucker.

OLLIE: Let's steal fags off my brother and smoke them in the park.

JACK: (*choking*) This is gross.

OLLIE: (*choking*) Yup, gross.

JACK: We should just vape.

Jack leans forward to kiss Ollie, Ollie pulls back.

JACK: Are you scared?

OLLIE: Terrified.

JACK: Me too.

They kiss.

(*to audience*) We tell no one, it's our secret. We sit together in French class and one time we hold hands under the table. Madame DuBois totally spots us and I'm bricking it, but she just smiles.

JACK: I think we should do it.

OLLIE: Already? It's a bit soon isn't it?

JACK: I don't think so, it's been a year.

OLLIE: But, in public?

JACK: That's the point.

They reach out and take one another's hand.

OLLIE: What if my Mum finds out? And Mikey?

JACK: We'll fight them, we'll fight the world.

They take a deep breath and step forward.

STUDENTS: Brown nosers!

               Green leggers!

               Purple headers!

               Oi, shut up.

               It's not funny anymore.

               And have you seen Drag Race? It takes real balls to sow your own dress.

Home.

SALLY: Are you sure you don't want more roast potatoes, Ollie?

OLLIE: No thanks Mrs D...oh, ok, thanks.

SALLY: You need feeding up.

Jack takes a deep breath.

JACK:	Ollie and me are boyfriends. And we want your blessing.
SALLY:	Blessing!? But you're only thirteen.
JACK:	There are other kids at school who're dating.
SALLY:	That's not the point.
JACK:	What's the point?

Pause

JACK:	Just say we have your support. Because we need it, we really need it.
SALLY:	Come on, Martin, say something!
JACK:	(*to audience*) We have Ben & Jerry's after the nut roast and everyone survives the meal, just.

Martin and Sally alone.

SALLY:	How old were we when we first kissed?
MARTIN:	Oh... er... I dunno...
SALLY:	You were fifteen, I was fourteen.
MARTIN:	Come on, that was different.
SALLY:	Different how?
MARTIN:	Well, we were...
SALLY:	Straight?

Silence.

SALLY:	If we had it, why can't they have it too?
JACK:	(*to audience*) I know in their ideal world I'd fall in love with a girl but I've got Ollie, and together we're invincible. At school we team up with Madame DuBois to start an anti-bullying campaign. Someone from Stonewall comes in and runs a workshop on LGBTQ+ issues, it's good, even though a bunch of parents complain about it. When Ollie and I turn sixteen we go to The Old Rose for a pint. It's a lovely place. Old Norman's there every now and again, he always says hello, and he's always got some banner with him or a flag, off to some sort of rally I guess.

Pub.

OLLIE:	26,000! Secret waterfall, cherry blossom aaand the fire mountain! So. Many. Coins!
JACK:	There isn't a fire mountain.
OLLIE:	Wanna bet?
JACK:	Douche.
OLLIE:	Did you see those pics of Orlando Bloom? Well hung isn't he. And pretty. But not as pretty as you.

He leans in and kisses Jack.

JACK:	(*to audience*) And everything's perfect, until…

Home.

SALLY:	Darling, sit down.
JACK:	I'm fine.
SALLY:	Just sit down.
JACK:	I'm f –
SALLY:	Jack, I spot continuity errors in *Eastenders*, I'm not an idiot.

He sits.

JACK:	Oh Mum... It's Ollie, it's over. He found someone else.
SALLY:	Oh Jack, I'm so sorry. Was he cheating on you?
JACK:	No! He... we just spoke, for ages, and he was so nice about it. He wants to be friends. But I don't want to be friends, I want to be boyfriends. It fucking sucks.
SALLY:	Language. Look, there will be more guys, Jack, I promise.
JACK:	But he was meant to be the one like you and Dad.
SALLY:	We became the one but it wasn't easy, it took a lot of work. Your Dad doesn't come from a long line of communicators or men who are emotionally expressive.
JACK:	Did you have anyone to talk about it with?

SALLY:	Well, I've got my friends I suppose, Barbara and I love a good natter.
JACK:	You can talk to me, Mum, if you want.
	(*to audience*) At breakfast the next day, Dad says…
MARTIN:	These eggs are… mmm.

Silent eating.

MARTIN:	I'm sorry, Jack, about Ollie, he was special.
JACK:	He was.
MARTIN:	Give yourself some time, to let your heart heal. But it will.

Revision with Gemma.

JACK:	I just thought we were destined to be a gay Romeo and Juliet.
GEMMA:	What, one poisoned and one stabbed.
JACK:	Ok, but without the death bit.
GEMMA:	Jack, there's more to life than romance.
JACK:	I know, I know, but the movies make it look so good, and the pop songs.
GEMMA:	Don't make me say it.
JACK:	What?
GEMMA:	If you can't love yourself/how in the hell you gonna love somebody else?

67

JACK: / how in the hell you gonna love somebody else?

GEMMA: Can I get an amen?

JACK: Amen. It's harder for gay guys though, you straights get to go dating all the time.

GEMMA: Us "straights", excuse me. Do you know the sorts of guys who ask me out? The sort who spend more time looking at my tits than my face and experience about one emotion a year.

Silence.

GEMMA: Are you even listening to me?

JACK: I am, I am, it's just... this is bigger than me isn't it?

GEMMA: Lol, I always forget how humble you are.

JACK: I mean, this is about everyone.

GEMMA: Yeah, we're all fucking bonkers.

JACK: (*to audience*) I get Cs in English and Geography, and a B in French. I'm well proud of that B. So is Madame DuBois...

MME DUBOIS: Oh Jack! What a clever boy! I always knew you 'ad it in you, I always knew (*she kisses him on both cheeks*).

JACK: (*to audience*) A little inappropriate but she is very French. After the summer Gemma goes off to Uni in Leeds and Ollie moves to London.

I think about Uni but I'm not ready yet, there's only so much Molière I want to read. I start working at The Old Rose, it's not so bad. I help them put on their first LGBTQQIAAPP2S disco night, it's good, people actually come! Still, when I want something a bit juicier I jump on the Megabus to...

The sound of cheesy pop music...

JACK: The Royal Vauxhall Tavern! There's cabaret, burlesque, a Harry Potter quiz night, it's got everything. And the people are always super friendly, they even smile!

GUY: Do you fancy another lemonade?

JACK: Yes please

GUY: Nothing stronger?

JACK: I'm alright.

GUY: I said you have nice eyes, didn't I, and an epic nose.

JACK: Haha, thanks! You're beautiful.

GUY: Can I kiss you?

JACK: I'd prefer to talk for a bit, if that's OK?

GUY: Of course...

Music stops.

JACK: We do end up kissing and in that moment it's enough. I get the late bus home and go to bed. Next morning Mum's waiting for me in the kitchen.

SALLY: It's old Norman, he passed away.

JACK: Oh Mum.

SALLY: He was 94, he had a good life and he died in his sleep, peaceful I think. He was a legend, wasn't he? All that stuff he did with the BLT.

JACK: The GLF, Gay Liberation Front.

SALLY: That's the one.

JACK: He was trying to make the world a better place, wasn't he?

SALLY: He was a fighter, just like a certain boy I know.

JACK: Maybe.

SALLY: Definitely.

JACK: Do you think I'm strong?

SALLY: More than you know.

JACK: I just... I wish someone had told me what was coming. No one ever prepared me for all the crap I've been through.

Pause

SALLY: I'm sorry.

JACK: Why?

SALLY: For being part of the fight you've had to face.
               I didn't know how much I didn't know but
               I'm learning now, trust me.

JACK: (*to audience*) Next Monday it's the funeral.
               And one of the first people I see is...

Ollie steps forward.

OLLIE: You look great.

JACK: So do you.

OLLIE: How are you?

JACK: Fine. Not fine.

OLLIE: I couldn't believe it, what a hero.

JACK: And now he's a legend. How's London?

OLLIE: Very London!

JACK: Where are you living?

OLLIE: Walthamstow.

JACK: Hipster.

OLLIE: I eat avocado toast everyday.

JACK: Are you seeing anyone?

OLLIE: No. Are you?

JACK: No.

OLLIE: I'm on a wait-list though, for NHS therapy.

JACK: Nice.

OLLIE: It's a long wait but I think it'll be worth it. It's not easy being gay, is it?

JACK: No.

Gemma arrives. She spots them talking and holds back. Sally approaches.

SALLY: Gemma.

GEMMA: Mrs D! Hi!

SALLY: It's so nice of you to come back.

GEMMA: Of course, poor Norman.

SALLY: Poor Norman. How's everything at university?

GEMMA: Good thanks, I've started writing a novel actually.

SALLY: Very impressive. And are you seeing anyone nice?

GEMMA: Yeah, me.

SALLY: What?

GEMMA: I'm dating myself, Mrs D. Life's too short for dysfunctional men taking their shit out on me.

GEMMA: It's hard though, being single, but I'm working on it. I'm telling the woman in the mirror that she's beautiful and clever, that she's enough. And I'm trying to believe it.

SALLY: You should because you are all those things, Gemma.

GEMMA: So are you Mrs D.

Gemma approaches Ollie and Jack.

GEMMA: My favourite boys!

OLLIE/JACK: Gemma!

GEMMA: When are we going to do a *Fantastic Beasts* marathon?

JACK: Never, I am boycotting those films.

OLLIE: Worse than *The Cursed Child*.

GEMMA: That bad? Ouch.

The sound of an organ, they take their seats.

VICAR: ...we commend to Almighty God our brother Norman; and we commit his body to the ground; earth to earth, ashes to ashes, dust to dust.

JACK/GEMMA/OLLIE: Amen.

Jack gets up.

JACK: I spoke to Norman on and off but I never really got to know him. I never asked him about the banners he was always carrying and the marches he went on. I guess I didn't really think it mattered. But it does because he was making the world a better place.

He takes out the time turner.

I grew up believing that gay meant shit. Dirty. Shameful. But before all of that, before it even meant homosexual, it meant happy.

Gemma steps forward.

GEMMA: Jack, are you going back again?

JACK: There's still so much more to do. I'm going to make friends with Norman, I'll go on marches with him, I'll petition the government.

GEMMA: Jack, you can't do everything.

JACK: But I've got to do something. I mean, someone's got to stop the TERFs.

GEMMA: And you should go vegan.

Ollie steps forward.

OLLIE: Vegan?

GEMMA: A meat reducer.

JACK: I just want a world in which queer kids can be happy. I want the suicide rate to be zero. (*to Ollie*) I don't want you to kill yourself. I don't want you to even think about doing it. *I* don't want to think about doing it. (*to Gemma*) And

I don't want you to get caught in the crossfire,
it isn't fair. I want us all to be happy. I want
this snake around my heart to uncoil and die,
like in *The Chamber of Secrets*.

OLLIE: I think you'll find it's a Basilisk.

JACK: Nerd.

OLLIE: Learnt from the best.

JACK: If I can just do half the things Norman did,
then I can change the world.

GEMMA: We. We can change the world.

OLLIE: You can't do this alone, Jack.

GEMMA: We're coming with you.

JACK: Really?

GEMMA: This isn't just about you anymore.

OLLIE: It's about everyone.

GEMMA: Besides, we love you.

JACK: I love you too.

Pause.

JACK: And one more thing.

GEMMA: What?

JACK: Dumbledore's going to live.

OLLIE: Damn straight. Damn gay. How many turns is it?

GEMMA: Three?

JACK: No, we're going to need a lot more than that.

END